Participants Notes

Sometimes life's the pits...

Our lives on a personal level

Our relationships

Our lives in society

Our lives on a global level

Are there any clues to the 'God' question?

The miracle of life

A world of design

The existence of our emotions

Our sense that there is a God

What could this God be like?

Bigger than time and space

Interested in the smallest detail

Never exhausting our exploration

Interested in us

Notes

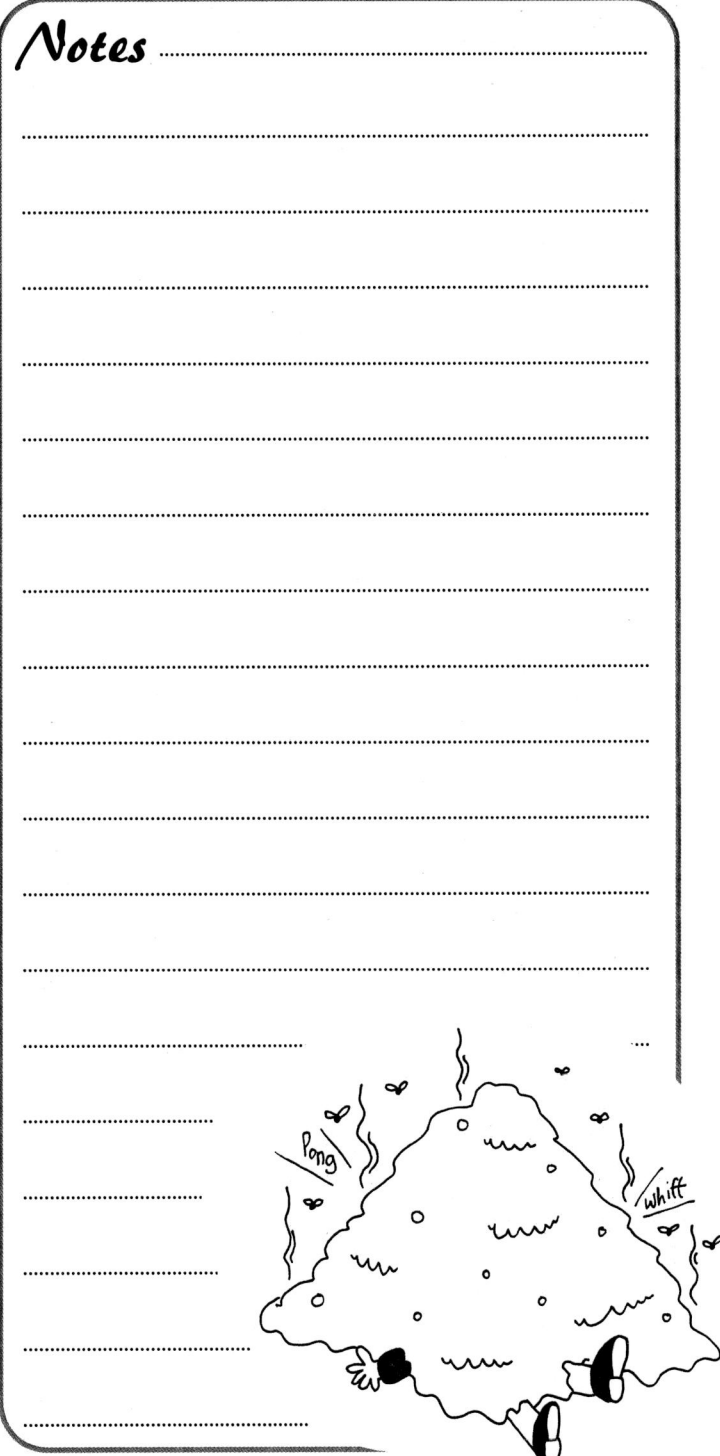

Does anybody know what we're living for?

Freddie Mercury

No rain, no mushrooms
No God, no world.

African proverb

Always, always, always
without relief there's this
black hole inside and
it never goes away.

Bob Geldof

I have ten pairs of
shoes - one for each
day of the week

Samantha Fox

I believe in the
Kingdom come,
when all the
colours bleed into
one but I
still haven't found
what
I'm looking for.

Bono (U2)

How can I believe in
God when just last
week I got my
tongue caught in the
roller of an electric
typewriter?

Woody Allen

Just like a tiny baby's body, so our planet, and our solar system, our galaxy, even beyond to the universe - all of it is infused not with randomness but with intricate and finely balanced design. All this design points to one obvious conclusion - a designer. It makes sense. Big Ben didn't just spring out of the ground. The beautifully created St Paul's Cathedral didn't appear in London one day. It had a gifted architect in the person of Sir Christopher Wren. This is equally true of the lovely Ferrari 355 F1 Spider. The awesome design both in body and engine had a whole team of technicians and planners behind it. In other words, it is unthinkable to have design without a designer.

from Beyond Belief? - by Peter Meadows &
Joseph Steinberg with Donna Vann

The problem of discovering what God is like

A limit to our knowledge

A limit to our reasoning power

A bias to our judgement

The only answer is for God to open the communication

Was Jesus more than a very good man?

His unique power and authority

His teaching focused on himself

He was all we could hope a God would be

Jesus made it clear he was God

He said he and God were the same

He spoke of having always existed

He forgave sin

He accepted the title 'Messiah'

The trilemma

Was Jesus a lunatic?

...a liar?

...or Lord?

Y - he came
Jesus was both fully God and fully human - explaining the impact of his unique life

Notes

Are you from Bob's Breakdown?

BOB'S BREAKDOWN

BOB

A child asks 'Why?' and 'How?' and 'Why?' again - and again. The parent has the answers and would love to be able to give them. But the child's reasoning power does not stretch far enough - to say the least. That's how it is when exploring the God agenda. Our brain power does not match the task. It's like asking the average six-year-old to grasp the intricacies of algebraic trigonometry. Only worse. In terms of our ability to wrap our minds around all that God entails, we are as sharp as marbles.

from Beyond Belief?

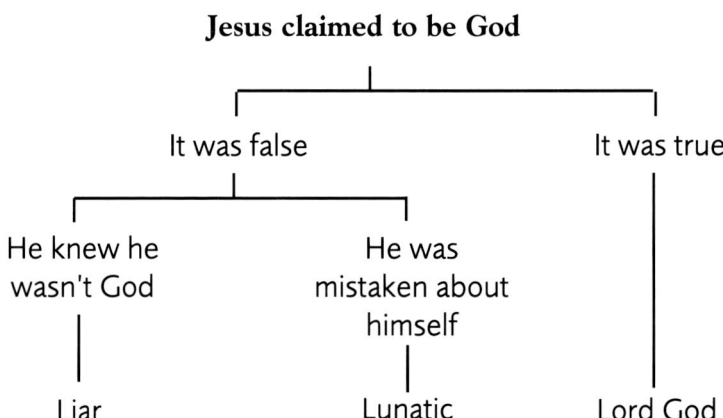

Jesus claimed to be God

It was false — It was true

He knew he wasn't God — He was mistaken about himself

Liar — Lunatic — Lord God

Who was this Jesus?

One day as Jesus was teaching, Pharisees and teachers of the law, who had come from every village of Galilee and from Judea and Jerusalem, were sitting there. And the power of the Lord was present for him to heal the sick.

Some men came carrying a paralytic on a mat and tried to take him into the house to lay him before Jesus. When they could not find a way to do this because of the crowd, they went up on the roof and lowered him on his mat through the tiles into the middle of the crowd, right in front of Jesus.

When Jesus saw their faith, he said, 'Friend, your sins are forgiven.'

The Pharisees and the teachers of the law began thinking to themselves, 'Who is this fellow who speaks blasphemy? Who can forgive sins but God alone?'

Jesus knew what they were thinking and asked, 'Why are you thinking these things in your hearts? Which is easier: to say, "Your sins are forgiven," or to say, "Get up and walk? But that you may know that the Son of Man has authority on earth to forgive sins. . . .' He said to the paralysed man, "I tell you, get up, take your mat and go home."

Immediately he stood up in front of them, took what he had been lying on and went home praising God. Everyone was amazed and gave praise to God. They were filled with awe and said, 'We have seen remarkable things today.'

- as told in Luke's account of Jesus' life

Are we expected to believe what happened so long ago?

Reasons to be confident in the Gospel records

It didn't happen in a corner

People kept the stories alive

Their memories were sharp

They wrote it down

The writers were not daft

Enemies were watching to catch them out

Lots of ancient copies exist

The issue has been thoroughly investigated

The recipe still works

Can it really be true that Jesus died and came back to life?

Was Jesus still alive when he left the cross?

Was it a grave mistake?

Was it all in the mind?

Did Jesus' followers die for a lie?

What transformed these ordinary people?

Notes

You got that wrong, Jesus didn't have a follower called Kevin!

	Was the tomb of Jesus really empty?				
Possible explanation	His followers stole the body	His followers went to the wrong tomb	The Jews or Romans stole the body	Jesus lived through the ordeal	Jesus had risen from the dead
Objection	But then they gave their lives for what they knew to be a lie	But then the Jews or Romans would have pointed out their mistake	But then they would have produced the body to silence the claim	But then he would have had to move a 2 ton stone and overcome trained Roman guards by himself	
Did the followers of Jesus really see him alive again?					
Possible explanation	They invented it on purpose	They saw a ghost or an illusion	They imagined it	Jesus had risen	
Objection	But then why were his dejected followers so transformed?	But then why were they able to touch him and how come he ate food with them?	But 500 people don't imagine the same thing all at the same time.		

That man Jesus

'That man was probably a failure in his own time....He taught in strange riddles. He didn't convince his fellow Jews. And he didn't overthrow Rome. From that failure I have come to what, for me, is the most important conclusion of all. That the hardest, apparently least historical article of Christian faith, the resurrection, must have happened. If there had been no miracle after Jesus' death, there would have been no grounds for faith in a failed life. No resurrection...no church.'

Mark Tully *at the end of his BBC TV series* Lives of Jesus

We've done it our way

The reality of sin

What sin does
    It spoils
    It separates

Y - the centre
*Our lives are meant to have
God at their centre*

Why can't God turn a blind eye?

Why the symbol of the cross?

What was his crime?

What Jesus said about his death
    It didn't take him by surprise
    It was for a specific purpose

The identity of Jesus is the key

What was the point of Jesus' death?
    Jesus was God's once-for-all-time sacrifice

The day the sun stopped shining

Three ways to respond
    The good way is to believe
    The bad way is to get religious about it
    The ugly way is to reject God's generous
       offer altogether

The difference that waits
    A clean slate
    A clear conscience
    A restored relationship

Notes

15

Have you ever found yourself in charge of a super-market trolley that spent its time crashing into stacks of food no matter how hard you tried to steer it? The symptoms of the problem can be seen in the dents made in people and produce. But it's the condition of the trolley that's the real problem.

from Beyond Belief?

Why was Jesus' death such a big deal when he knew he would come back to life?

In one sense this was an everlasting night. For a God who lives outside of time, those hours on the cross will last forever. Those wounds of Jesus will never heal....
And he did it all for us – to make our forgiveness possible.

from Beyond Belief?

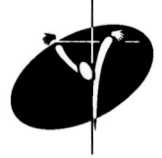

Y - the cross
Through his death Jesus made forgiveness possible for everyone

The fulfilment of prophecy

One of the most remarkable things about Jesus is the way his birth, life and death accurately fulfilled prophecies made centuries before he was born.

The following list is just a small selection of over 300 such prophecies recorded in Jewish religious writings.

- Born in Bethlehem

- Born of a virgin

- Betrayed by a friend

- Beaten and spat upon after his arrest

- Hands, feet & body pierced

- Lots cast for his clothes at his execution

- No bones broken

- Buried in rich man's tomb

- Would rise again from the dead

Why so many religions and so much suffering?

The major world faiths have contributed much to our lives and cultures

Are all religions the same?
>What kind of God do they have?
>How do they keep God on their side?

Do all religions lead to God?

Isn't sincerity enough?

What does Jesus say about other religions?

What makes Jesus so different from the founders of other religions?

There's too much suffering to believe

>We share the blame

>God allows us the dignity of human choice

>We live in a spoiled world

>Our understanding is limited

>God responds to our pain

>A mystery still remains

Notes

Don't all roads lead to God?

God is not a city - God is a person. If he were a city we could approach him on any given road. But, as a person, he is reached only through a relationship - and on his terms.

'God has feelings, views, expectations, likes and dislikes - and relates to us on that basis. A city has character, not personality. So while the city limits sign may say 'Welcome' it doesn't have a heart that leaps for joy when you get there.

from Beyond Belief?

God is powerful enough to remove all evil from the earth, if that's the way he wanted to play it. But would you want it? Do you fancy living in a place like Seahaven, the TV-location-city featured in the Jim Carrey film 'The Truman Show'? This controlled environment was populated by people pushing baby carriages, riding bicycles, and cleaning their spotless houses in exactly the same way every day for all of the time. And all presided over by the watchful benevolent producer-God.

For everyone in Seahaven except Truman, this was adequate - because they were actors. But Truman...was a real, living human with needs and desires and frustations, which eventually made him yearn to break out of the perfect world.

We can't have it both ways. Either we will be in Seahaven as robots living according to the script, or on a planet where we are allowed the dignity of choice. And once we get to choose, sometimes we will choose harm - to ourselves and others.

from Beyond Belief?

The Long Silence

At the end of time, billions of people were scattered on a great plain before God's throne. Most shrank back from the brilliant light before them. But some groups near the front talked heatedly - not with cringing shame, but with belligerence. Can God judge us? What does he know about suffering?

Far out across the plain there were hundreds of such groups. Each had a complaint against God for the evil and suffering he had permitted in his world. How lucky God was to live in heaven where everything was sweetness and light, where there was no weeping or fear, no hunger or hatred. What did God know of all that the human race had been forced to endure? For God leads a pretty sheltered life, they said.

So each of these groups sent out a leader, chosen because he or she had suffered most... In the centre of the plain they consulted with each other. At last they were ready to present their case. It was rather clever.

Before God could be qualified to be their judge, he must endure what they had endured. They decided that God should be sentenced to live on earth - as a man! 'Let him be born a Jew. Let people think him illegitimate. Give him a work so difficult that even his family would think him out of his mind when he tried to do it. Let him be betrayed by his closest friends. Let him face false charges, be tried by a prejudiced jury and convicted by a cowardly judge. Let him be beaten and tortured. At the last, let him see what it means to be terribly alone. Then let him die. Let him die so that there can be no doubt that he died. Let there be a host of witnesses to his death.'

As each leader announced his or her portion of the sentence, loud murmurs of approval went up from the throng of people assembled. When the last person had finished pronouncing sentence, there was a long silence. No-one uttered a word. No one moved. For suddenly all knew that God had already served his sentence.

quoted in Beyond Belief?

What happens when we die?

What did Jesus say about life after death?
>Heaven is a place where he is
>It's forever
>It's a great place to be
>It's a place for those who have pre-registered

Our future depends on the issue of forgiveness
>Today's choices matter forever

Can we count on Jesus to lead us home?

What faith isn't

Three kinds of faith
>Automatic faith
>Dependent or sustaining faith
>Saving faith

It is what our faith is in that matters

Faith involves action

Simple steps to saving faith
>A realisation of need
>A decision to seek forgiveness
>A turning from the mess of the past
>A dependence on the mercy of the Father
>An acceptance of the offer of forgiveness
>A life as a child not a servant

The faith transaction

There may be barriers to believing

The scene at heaven's gate

Notes

Y - the choice
The road of life demands a decision.
And Jesus said, 'I am the way.'

A Prayer

Dear Lord God

I am overwhelmingly in debt to you because of my sin. Because of what I am and what I have done, I have hurt you, damaged others and spoilt your world.

I would like a new start and am now turning away from all I know to be wrong and setting my feet on the path to follow you.

Thank you that Jesus died on the cross to pay the price for my sin. I now receive the gift of your forgiveness that this made possible.

Please take hold of my life as my Lord and come and live your life in me forever.

Thank you for hearing this prayer and for answering it.

There is no world beyond our own, of this we can be sure. Any goldfish will tell you

What Jesus said to someone about to die

Two other men, both criminals, were also led out with him to be executed. When they came to the place called the Skull, there they crucified him, along with the criminals — one on his right, the other on his left.

One of the criminals who hung there hurled insults at him: 'Aren't you the Christ? Save yourself and us!' But the other criminal rebuked him. 'Don't you fear God,' he said, 'since you are under the same sentence? We are punished justly, for we are getting what our deeds deserve. But this man has done nothing wrong.'

Then he said, 'Jesus, remember me when you come into your kingdom.' Jesus answered him, 'I tell you the truth, today you will be with me in paradise.'

as told in Luke's account of Jesus life

Disciple - the job description is 'apprentice'
>   Disciples are ready to give up their life
>   Disciples are ready to let go
>   Disciples are obedient

Behaving like a disciple doesn't get you to heaven

Don't try to go it alone
>   They're out to get us

Back to the factory

God in three persons

The Father - the perfect parent
>   He loves us no matter what
>   He's at work on our behalf

The Son - the image of the Father
>   He holds us in his grasp

The Holy Spirit - our helper
>   He reminds us of what we heard
>   He teaches us what we need to learn
>   He gives us the power we need
>   He helps us be sure we are God's child

A final question

Notes

....

....

....

....

....

....

....

....

....

Y - the change
We can be transformed by the loving forgiveness of a heavenly father

As we journey onward from that door of forgiveness, God's not encouraging us from the sidelines like a parent at a school sports day. Enthusiastic, caring, but powerless. Instead he's actually running in our shoes.

I remember watching my son Joel zoom round a racing track at the wheel of a high-powered sports car. The experience was an eighteenth birthday gift. I was impressed - until his instructor changed places with him and took control. Then we saw what could be done and the motoring really began. But it was only possible because the one who could make the difference was in the driving seat.

And that's where we need God to be at work. Within us. At the very heart of all we are.

from Beyond Belief?

The decision to seize hold of God's offer of forgiveness by faith is vastly more significant than making up your mind to switch your brand of deodorant or to show up in church more often. It demands even more than changing your allegiance to a football team or taking a decision to become a vegetarian.

from Beyond Belief?

8 Who wants to be stuck with a bunch of boring old rules?

There is nothing we can do to earn God's love

Rules are not God's plan
> Rule-keeping is based on pride and rejects
> God's love

If not rules, what?
> A living relationship
> Accepted as we are

What about when we fail?
> Restoring the relationship
> Can we do what we like and then say sorry?

Nurturing our relationship with God

> **It's good to talk**
> > *Prayer is not a ritual, it's a conversation*

> **Food for thought**
> > *Read chunks at a time*
> > *Read with a willingness to discover and act*
> > *Memorise some of it*
> > *Read it with others*

> **Be ready to pollinate**
> > *Don't get up people's noses*

> **Join a fragrant bunch**
> > *There's strength in numbers*

The big picture

Notes

Jesus was all we could hope a God would be.

If God walked the earth, what would you want him to be like? And to what extent does Jesus match it?

Jesus was compassionate. Faced with a widowed mother whose only son, and her sole means of support had died, Jesus raised him to life. Face to face with lepers, the AIDS victims of the day, he did the unthinkable and touched them.

Jesus left no one out. Prostitutes, people who lived on the edge of society, social outcasts were all welcomed by him. And women, the underclass of the day, received special affirmation and dignity from the way he treated them.

Jesus made ordinary people feel comfortable in his presence. There was nothing super-religious or stand-offish about him. Children swarmed round his feet, he was a welcome guest at a wedding, he enjoyed a normal social life.

Jesus detested religious hypocrisy. He spoke out against those with a better-than-thou attitude. Religion for the show of it stuck in his throat - and he said so.

Jesus welcomed those ready for a new start. He never wrote people off. A prostitute, a thief and collaborator with the occupying enemy for example all received the chance to start again. No one was too far gone for him to love them.

from Beyond Belief?

Discussion Questions

Some of these questions may be used in your group.

Box 1:

> **When you hear the word "God" what first comes to your mind?**
>
> a.   A remote force who made everything
>
> b.   Superman
>
> c.   A friend who listens
>
> d.   Father Christmas
>
> e.   A loving father who forgives
>
> f.   Nothing
>
> g.   The big boss out there somewhere
>
> h.   A judge out for revenge on people who do wrong
>
> i.   A mother who cares and understands
>
> j.   Someone who holds everything in their hands
>
> k.   Other _____

Box 2:

> **What do you see as the most convincing clue that God exists?**
>
> a.   Such a complex universe could not have happened by accident.
>
> b.   Where else could our emotions and sense of justice have come from?
>
> c.   I've always had a sense that there is a God.
>
> d.   People have always believed in a God.
>
> e.   None of them.
>
> f.   Other _____

Box 3:

How do you tend to see yourself in relation to God at this point in your life?

a. I don't.

b. At a distance expressing interest.

c. By his desk waiting instructions.

d. Outside his door asking to come in.

e. In his arms being protected and loved.

f. At the end of a phone having a conversation

g. Lost but looking for directions.

h. Pass

i. Other_____

Box 4:

Which two of the following seem to you the most convincing proof that Jesus did come alive again?

a. Jesus said he would.

b. He was seen after his death by many groups of people at many different times.

c. If his body was still around, the Roman rulers or the Jewish authorities would have produced it.

d. Those who were convinced it was true believed strongly enough to die for their convictions.

e. He cooked breakfast for a group of his closest friends and spent a long time talking with them.

f. His followers never expected it to happen yet became totally convinced that it had.

g. Those who knew him well saw him, touched him, recognised him and spoke with him.

h. If it hadn't happened there was no need for his followers to invent it.

Box 5:

What comes to your mind when you hear the word 'sin' or 'sinner'?

a. Old fashioned views about right and wrong

b. Things like murder or robbery

c. Something other people do

d. Bad people who should be in prison

e. Ordinary human failure

f. Other_____

Box 6:

Most people think you get to heaven by being good. Which of the following do you think best expresses why this can't be true?

a. A perfect heaven would become tainted by us being any thing less than perfect. So 'good' is not good enough.

b   If being good got us to heaven then the death of Jesus must have been a mistake.

c. How could anyone know when 'good' is good enough?

d. Jesus said his death was to be a 'ransom' which means he needed to rescue us because our goodness couldn't do it.

Box 7:

What do you think would have been the greatest challenge to those who heard Jesus at the time in terms of what he asked of them?

a. Letting go of their self-centred plans

b. Behaving as though Jesus was the most important person in their life.

c. The prospect of having to stand out in the crowd

d. Making sure their possessions did not get in the way of their relationship with God

Box 8:

For someone who has made the step of saving faith, what do you think would make it hard for them to be certain they are now fully forgiven and are God's child forever?

a. That they may not feel any different.

b. That they may have a sense of not being good enough.

c. That nothing dramatic may have happened.

d. That there was still so much to know.

e. That it seems arrogant to make such a claim.

f. That it's all rather complicated.

g. Other _____

....

....

....

....

....

....

....

....

....

....

....

....

....

....